FAITH
or manifestation

faith ~~fake~~ it
until you
make it

Dr Nathalie Turgeon Ph.D.

All rights reserved. This book may not be reproduced in whole or in part, stored in a retrieval system, or transmitted in any form or by any means electronic, mechanical, or other without written permission of the author, except by reviewer, who may quote brief passages with source information in a review.

Cover and interior design: Nathalie Turgeon
ISBN: 978-1-7380358-5-4
ISBN version française: 978-1-7380358-4-7

Faith or manifestation

For several years now we have been hearing about manifestation. And for those who have decided to reject any aspect of religion and spirituality, this concept of manifestation is attractive and appealing. Some have great success in seeing their desires and dreams manifest while for others, something of the concept seems to be missing in their equation. They expect to find a miracle formula. They expect a power within them to emerge and to allow them to create miracles. They approach the concept with their intellect and hope to find the complete equation only with an intellectual point of view or an ego one.

We see more and more people coming from the 'world of science' making connections with spirituality. Of course, what is most conveyed by these people are the more scientific portions, but when we take the time to read their works and watch the documentaries that they have created with their extensive research, we can very well see that the spiritual aspect has a large place in the equation that they demonstrate.

    I don't know if you have seen it before, there is a post that's been circulating on social media for several years that mentions that from a religious perspective, we use the word spirit, from a scientific perspective, we use the word energy, and from an everyday perspective in the street, we use the word vibe. And it concludes by saying that no matter what, when you feel it, follow it. Although inaccurate because even in spirituality we use the word energy, the first time I saw it, I thought it was good because it allows everyone to find what they're looking for, and at the same time it opens a door in the conscious mind to be curious and know more. Many people prefer to never use vocabulary with religious connotations for their own personal reasons. However, when we talk about manifestation, energy, vibe, and the invisible, we are still referring to faith.

Faith or manifestation

For most people, having faith means believing in something before you can even see it. And often, this concept in everyday life is difficult to accept, let alone master.

I would like to tell you that having faith does not mean blindly believing in something first and then seeing it. But I would also like to tell you that having faith is indeed blindly believing in something because yes, you have to believe without the ego being part of the equation, without the intellect intervening in the process or veiling a portion of the process of faith.

For the intellect it is an impossible concept, and I will explain why in all simplicity.

Faith or manifestation

When I was younger, I would have liked someone to explain the process to me rather than teaching me and repeating to me without explanation that faith is believing before seeing, and that someone who is not able to believe without seeing does not have faith (in God). Nonsense!

This erroneous way of thinking and believing continues to sow doubt today and continues to distance people from their full power, their spiritual well-being, and their physical well-being. Often, even their inner connection is broken because they cannot see beyond this belief. And guess what? This is exactly what pleases the ego or the intellect depending on the vocabulary you prefer.

Faith or manifestation

Look at this image before I continue.

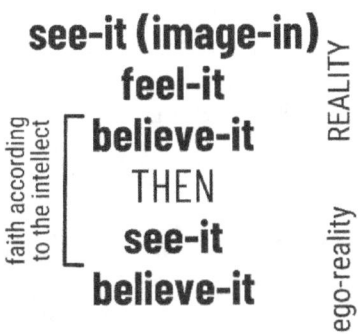

Can you see that the *I-have-to-see-it-to-believe-it* portion is actually just a portion of the whole? And can you also see that the process of manifestation is actually just the process of faith?

The intellect can only believe what it sees, hears, touches, smells, feels, tastes, so with the senses of the

Faith or manifestation

physical body the intellect makes a truth. Everything that is seen, heard, touched, smelled, felt, tasted becomes data that is recorded in a personal database called the subconscious. To change a truth, the intellect must have new data replacing the old data in the personal database, in the subconscious.

The intellect or ego must therefore see to believe since what is not in the subconscious is not a truth, so it falls into the category of what is impossible. We surely all know the saying: *I will believe it when I see it*.

But why must the ego see to believe?

Because the ego, or intellect, takes its information from the database where everything is recorded.

Because the ego, or intellect, belongs to the physical body and its surrounding reality.

Because when humans face a situation, no matter what it is, the intellect gathers data in the mental space, known as the mind-in our mind, to know how to face it and know how to react or re-act. It is not for nothing that there are often several weeks of practice before a dress rehearsal, or that people who have jobs that require a lot of precision have had several years of practice before starting their career. These practices mean that when the time comes, the person is not faced with the unknown or the impossible since the necessary data is in their database, in their subconscious ready to resurface in the mental space. The physical body being a device for the mind, it responds and re-acts or knows how to act. Often without having to think again or act blindly.

Our ego, or our intellect, is very important for our survival. When the ego gathers data taken from our database, it is to easily and quickly survive the present situation.

Therefore, everything we have experienced and are experiencing is recorded in our subconscious. Our DNA is also part of it since it is data, different but still data of functioning and non-functioning. Our beliefs and non-beliefs, our personal, collective, and cultural limitations, our habits of thinking and acting, our emotions associated with what they are associated with are all data that are part of our subconscious.

And the more we take the same data to face a situation, a conversation, an imagination, the more this data remains active. This must be seen in the same way as practices before a general. The more we practice, the more movements and words become fluid and sometimes even unconsciously. Take the example of driving a car. How many have already experienced going from point A to point B, lost in thoughts without realizing the streets turned by habit and the highway exits taken by habit. Even the physical body knows what to do and how to react to brake and accelerate or put on a turn signal while you are completely lost in your thoughts.

The more a data is fed, the more it grows and is the one that will be the first taken the next time a similar situation arises, or a thought of this or that person or this, or that thing resurfaces. Automatically. Why? To know how to react. To be able to survive what is and will be. It is the ego that controls the mental space.

The ego has seen, and it has believed, so as long as it continues to see what it believes, it will continue to believe in what it sees. This cycle reinforces the data and justifies that it is true. Why stop believing in something that is confirmed every time, right?

And as long as the ego controls the mental space with this data *I-saw-therefore-I-believe*, the person will always be in re-action mode and will move forward in their life by default or in survival mode.

The more a person gets used to what has been seen as their truth, the more they will think that it is difficult to believe something that has never been seen or heard, read, or felt. Meaning having faith. Because it comes out of their reality and enters into the abstract or metaphysics, everything that is beyond the physical.

To simplify what follows, let us say that the ego belongs to the human being as the soul belongs to the spiritual being. We are all spiritual or energetic beings experiencing through physical beings. The physical body is therefore a device for the mind, although most people will use another often heard saying which is that the body is a vehicle for the soul.

I add here that the ego with its ego-personality functions in its ego-reality. The ego-personality is the person that we are that changes or not over time at the same time as the reality that surrounds us, our ego-reality.

In the linear world that has a past, a present and a future, this present is actually just filled with data from the past to re-act and therefore move forward by default. Which makes each day or each phase of life more or less repeated. More or less because if new data is added voluntarily with full awareness, tomorrow or the next phase will have a new design.

Why? Because there will have been a modification or replacement of the data in the database, in the subconscious. Which means that when something happens, the information to deal with it will no longer be the same as before, so the actions will also be different. The stories fed into the mind will also be different.

And if a person understands that the present moment contains the past, the present and the future simultaneously, each day can become a new whole since this person moves outside of their ego-comfort zone. And it is with faith that a person can get out of this ego-comfort zone.

This is where understanding and having faith can become very important.

The ego or intellect only has access to what is tangible or visible, or let's say part of human life. The ego does not have access to data that is beyond the physical senses. That is why when we think of something, until it is felt, said, written or seen, it remains only static images that pass through the mind that do not come to life in any way. They have no value until we give it value, that is, until the ego gives it value.

So, it is the thoughts that are thought or reflected that take shape because we give them life first in our mental space. An image that is accompanied by emotions is an image that comes to life.

Emotion is what fuels the image. Sometimes, the image does not generate emotions, but by dint of seeing and re-seeing it, one or more details are accompanied by emotions since the intellect is looking for something similar in our database allowing us to feel something pleasant or not. When we see something several times, therefore again and again, the intellect has more time to appropriate all the details and give it more and more life. It becomes many practices before a general one. Hence the importance of stopping feeding in our mental space what we do not want to experience.

Remember the process.

Faith or manifestation

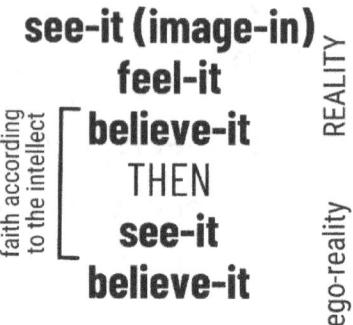

Now, I am going to tell you something that will make it easier to understand all this: the intellect or the ego believes that everything in the subconscious is true regardless of its origin. And we know that the most active data is that which quickly surfaces in the mental space to face of a current situation. One of the roles of the ego is our survival and it takes its role very seriously.

But the data in our subconscious does not only come from our physical experience. It also comes from our Higher Self and the Higher Consciousness. So, the more time you take to connect to your Higher Self, the more you leave room for your full potential to add data to your subconscious, therefore, to believe it and then eventually see it.

I may seem to be stepping away from the topic of faith, but this portion will ensure that the questions coming from the ego that must see to believe are silenced.

Take the time to look at the following image which is part of another of my publications. It is more or less complete, but what is necessary is present to better understand.

Faith or manifestation

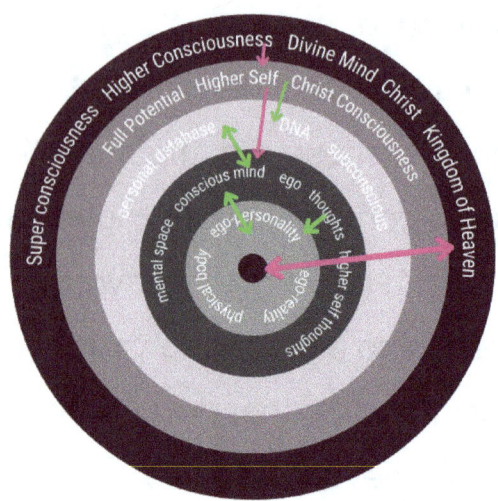

- The body is an instrument for the conscious mind. It only reproduces or responds.
- Everything that enters the mental space through the physical senses is recorded in the database, in the subconscious.
- The Christ Consciousness through the Higher Self impresses or adds information into the subconscious.
- The ego or intellect only has access to the database and what it contains, regardless of where the data comes from.
- The conscious mind searches for its information in the database. This information has no power, it is passive data.
- The conscious mind is the space to choose what to do with the information that surfaces.
- The ego, Higher Self or Christ Consciousness can control mental space and the choice of information.

Faith or manifestation

So, when it comes to having faith in something, it does not mean hoping for something impossible or unimaginable. It means taking the time to sit down and complete the process voluntarily and with full awareness. We must take the time to meditate or pray in silence, which is the same thing. A little parenthesis here on prayer: many believe that asking and begging is what prayer is. In fact, prayer is a conversation within oneself in which we participate in the co-creation of something. We take the time to connect to our infinite being, to listen to the Higher Consciousness, to be receptive to inspired actions and to be in gratitude mode for what will be. So, we must take the time to review the process of manifesting what we desire or need

Faith or manifestation

from beginning to end without the ego intervening. We must activate our faith.

Too often we try to believe in something we would like to see, but the ego veils that we have already seen it before so as not to activate the data and of course, bring the images to life with our emotions.

We must lift up the ego veils to go beyond, where the ego cannot go. Since the physical body cannot access the non-tangible or non-visible world since it uses the eyes of the human body and the physical senses, it is therefore with the senses of our energetic being that we can access the non-visible. This is what we call our clairs like clairvoyance, clairsentience, clairaudience, claircognizance. These are the senses that become active when we close our eyes and detach ourselves from the feelings of our physical body. This has nothing to do with magic. It is quite logical to think that if our physical being has senses, our energetic or spiritual being has some too.

If you close your eyes, you can more easily imagine, that is having a mental image, although some people cannot imagine, and others have a very vivid and colorful imagination.

When we imagine something, it is in our mental space that we see it. Whether it is an image or even words. Whether it is pleasant or not. It is in the mental space that it happens. And when we take the time to feed this imagination, we add the energy that this imagination needs to be set in motion and come to fruition. When we see an image and we feel what it represents or what it is for us, these emotions felt come to validate the image. These emotions confirm that we are beginning to believe in what we see as a possibility. And the more we imagine it with emotions, the more we are convinced that it can happen and be real. Again, whether it is pleasant or not.

And if we believe it long enough and imagine it often, we even end up acting following up on this imagination. It begins to take shape and becomes reality. Sometimes, the actions are logical and intellectualized and sometimes they are inspired.

Faith or manifestation

So, what we saw in our mental space, which we fed with increasingly strong and constant and continuous emotions, we believed it to the point that it became true for us, and when it became visible in our ego-reality, we can only believe it beyond any doubt. In fact, I say ego-reality because in our imagination, in our mental space, in the non-visible it was already a reality.

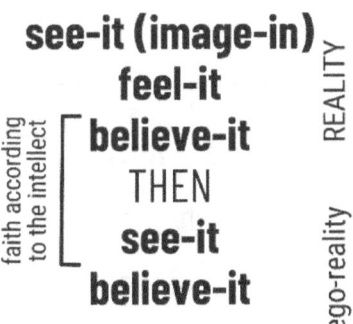

So, as you see, faith is not and has never been anything other than believing to see. It is an ego-conception to keep us away from our full potential and our full power of co-creation.

The ego is not a winner when we take the time to feed our imagination positively and wisely, because at that moment we become the designer of our future.

When ideas come from our full potential or our Higher Self, and they are inspired by the Higher Consciousness to allow us to be happy, because God (Source, Divine Mind, Infinite Intelligence, Higher Consciousness) only wants our well-being and happiness, the path to follow is open without ego-effort. And since the ego cannot access the non-visible, but only what is in its database to project what can be and exist, its equation therefore begins with *I-must-see-to-believe*. Its control in our mental space seeks to occupy all our time to keep us from taking the time to meditate, to pray, to connect within where the ego cannot follow.

We have just seen that nothing exists before it has been seen. Everything that exists was first an idea, a thought and an image that was seen, and reviewed, and felt and felt again, with a desired result. Even when we do not fully understand the how and why. It is a process that is sometimes quick or even instantaneous and sometimes can extend over several decades. We have seen it with the invention of airplanes, car engines, electricity, computers that communicate with each other from one end of the planet to the other. A painter's canvas, a sculpture, a dress, a table, a house, everything was seen in the mental space before becoming a tangible and possible reality. These people had faith and followed their inner guidance.

So having faith is not believing before seeing, but rather not following the path and logic of the ego or the intellect; it is to see in oneself, to believe it with conviction through our felt emotions... before seeing it exist in our life... and to believe it again or confirm the belief.

Faith or manifestation

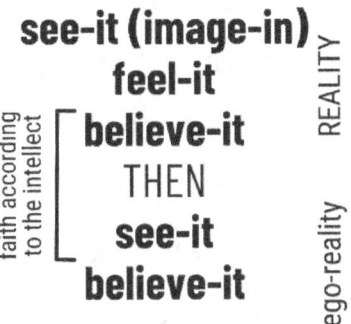

Many teach how to co-create or manifest only to please the ego, therefore, to improve their lives yes, but without necessarily making a difference, without following their full potential. These people therefore do not speak of faith because they are separated from their entirety or believe that it is a new process that has nothing to do with it.

It is in fact faith that is simply named with a more modern vocabulary to avoid triggering the ego which only seeks to keep its control and to limit its ego-comfort zone. It is also a way of allowing expansion without old religious connotations. And in our era, many have stepped away from religion but have at the same time rejected their spirituality. And since it is impossible to reject our essence, therefore the spiritual or energetic being that we are, a method of co-creation remains essential to the expansion of who we are and of the greater than oneself.

The ego or the intellect cannot let us believe correctly what faith is because that is what leads to its loss, to the loss of its control over our tomorrow. When we have faith, we believe in our full potential, in our power of co-creation with Higher Consciousness, the Divine Mind, Source or God, whatever you prefer to call this Creative Energy. And when we regain control of our mental space, we can change the destiny that the ego was happy to trace in front of us from old data. The faith that allows us to move mountains or walk on water, or to suddenly heal, it was not blind, it was imagined therefore seen in the mental space; it was felt with conviction and beyond any doubt therefore it was believed, then it was ego-true. Faith is what is true in reality before being true in ego-reality.

The Grand Masters were not going to meditate or pray to beg for a miracle, they were going to meditate to connect to align themselves beyond any doubt, or without their ego control with this first portion of seeing it, feeling it,

Faith or manifestation

and believing it to then co-create it. This creative force is not that of the ego or the human, it comes from the Higher Consciousness that creates through us.

The intellect cannot create anything by itself. It can only project what already exists.

Faith is the process of creation.

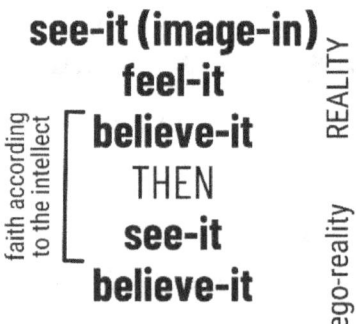

Looking at the picture from a new angle, we can see that not only is faith important, but it is the basis to follow.

Many people follow this process without even being aware of it.

Why do some affirmations or prayers work while others do not? Why do some desires manifest while others do not? Why do some unwanted things manifest anyway? Why do some people seem to experience miracles while others do not? Why do some things seem to persist and do more harm than good?

Because in the imagination and thoughts, therefore in the mental space, these desired or unwanted things are maintained and can only complete their process. What is in reality ends up in the ego-reality unless we act as an architect to change the plan at its base; unless we are aware of it and modify the data and only follow inspired actions, therefore those that come from the Higher Self.

The ego believes itself to be all-powerful and does everything in its power to keep its false beliefs active. And it is by lifting up the ego veils, that is to say by transmuting one by one the thoughts and beliefs of our ego that we can arrive at seeing beyond these veils. Therefore, to see with our soul, or our Higher Self or our full potential. It is by lifting up the ego veils that we can see this Light shining and illuminating our steps. The ego has everything to its advantage to make us believe that it is difficult to have faith. And now that you know that you can believe without seeing because you know the portion that comes before... you can firmly say that you have faith.

faith
~~fake~~ it
until you
make it

Dr. Nathalie Turgeon Ph.D.
Metaphysical Practitioner
Life coaching . Spiritual Coaching

Embodying her life mission

    Dr. Nathalie fully embodied her life mission when she decided to self-publish her first workbook in 2016. With no professional writing experience, she only knew that she had to start embodying her life mission in a different way. Believing in herself. Trusting herself and trusting the process. She always knew that writing and teaching was her passion.

    It is when she clearly understood her personal life mission that she jumped without a net, or rather with only a divine net as her only net in order to embody it by aligning herself with the one she knew she could become, and this, despite a more or less clear action plan veiled by her ego-based mind.

    Through gratitude and through her personal trials and personal life lessons which allowed her to become an expert in the art of remaining herself and of expressing her pleasure and her unconditional Love, she learned to develop an unconditional Gratitude Attitude and maintain it despite any current situations. It is this teaching method that she created with her Inner Self, which she received like a download when it was time to prepare the content of a workshop that she started sharing how she had achieved this unconditional Gratitude Attitude. She then brought it into an asynchronous online program and also as a book form. She also made gratitude the topic of her dissertation for her doctorate in philosophy, specializing in metaphysical counselling entitled: *Gratitude as a Spiritual Mind Treatment for Mental Health*.

While many get a doctorate degree and start working into their new career choice, she has already been enjoying metaphysics for more than twenty years before earning her Ph.D. Through her parallel career path as a Global Health Therapist while keeping one foot in the business office world she fully enjoyed, the one link she followed was the energy field one; from her working experience as a Naturopath combined to a Massage therapist practice, which inspired her to learn and become a Reiki Master while enjoying mystic fun practices like numerology and card readings and geomancy, it is once she became a Reiki Master that things started to unfold with a faster speed connecting all the dots, hence the importance of following inspirations even when we do not yet see the interconnection.

Her unconditional Gratitude Attitude would have not been possible without a personal Inner connection through lots of meditation and Inner work over many decades. While she was not teaching meditation per se, Dr. Nathalie did her master's thesis on meditation: "*Reaching the summit of consciousness through meditation like Great Masters and prophets did.*" She also self-published a Oneness affirmations book titled "*Self-realization Food for thoughts*"; 21 verses of powerful Oneness affirmations co-written with her Self that she was inspired to share.

Because she likes to learn and simplify things so that the ego-based mind does not interfere too much when learning different concepts or when the time comes to demystify the ego, and because one of her dreams is to allow everyone to have access to spiritual or metaphysical development and personal development information regardless of their budget and preferred method, she follows her inspirations by creating content to help people on their mindfulness journey by helping them from awareness to awakening, to then move from their awakening to reality allowing them to continue from an attitude of gratitude to Unity, to this interconnectivity and harmony with the Universe and the primary Source of the Universe.

Her teachings make it possible to understand that it is all a matter of understanding your ego so that you can lift up the ego veils, see from your Soul to choose your ego-identity aligned with your desires, and have an unconditional gratitude attitude. Through her personal experiences, she walked the talk and became an ego-based mind expert.

While she is having fun creating online content and books and workbooks for her personal development and spiritual well-being series, she continues to learn year after year by being herself on the front line in what she teaches. Her integrity comes from teaching only what she has learned to master herself in order to create a real personal and collective impact.

Her tag line that she received as not only a download but also as her teaching to help you with is...

Breathe in, let go of your ego-based mind thoughts and vision, see from your Soul, and Love Out!

breatheinloveoutcenter.ca

www.ingramcontent.com/pod-product-compliance
Lightning Source LLC
Chambersburg PA
CBHW052207070526
44585CB00017B/2105